INSTANT WEATHER FORECASTING

Also by Alan Watts

Air Rider's Weather

Basic Windcraft

Cruising Weather

Dinghy and Boardsailing Weather

Instant Storm Forecasting

Instant Wind Forecasting

Reading the Weather: Modern Techniques for Yachtsmen

Sailing off the Beach

The Seabreeze Handbook

Weather Forecasting Ashore and Afloat

The Weather Handbook

Weather Wise

Wind and Sailing Boats

The Wind Pilot

ADLARD COLES
Bloomsbury Publishing Plc
50 Bedford Square, London, WC1B 3DP, UK
Bloomsbury Publishing Ireland Limited,
29 Earlsfort Terrace, Dublin 2, D02 AY28, Ireland

BLOOMSBURY, ADLARD COLES and the Adlard Coles logo are trademarks of Bloomsbury Publishing Plc

First published in Great Britain 1968
Second edition 2000
Third edition 2007
Fourth edition 2011
Fifth edition 2016
This edition published 2026

A catalogue record for this book is available from the British Library

Library of Congress Cataloguing-in-Publication data has been applied for

ISBN: PB: 978-1-3994-3078-4; ePub: 978-1-3994-3076-0; ePDF: 978-1-3994-3075-3

2 4 6 8 10 9 7 5 3 1

Typeset in Futura and Helvetica Neue by Mark Bowerman

Printed and bound in China by C&C Offset Printing Co., Ltd.

To find out more about our authors and books visit www.bloomsbury.com and sign up for our newsletters

For product safety related questions contact productsafety@bloomsbury.com

INSTANT WEATHER FORECASTING

6th edition

A 24 colour photograph guide to weather forecasting from the clouds, for use by walkers, farmers, fishermen, yachtsmen, golfers, holidaymakers – in fact for anyone to whom the weather in the near future is of vital importance.

Alan Watts and Simon Keeling

LONDON • OXFORD • NEW YORK • NEW DELHI • SYDNEY

Contents

Preface to the Sixth Edition

Alan Watts was what I call a 'proper' weather forecaster. He knew his subject inside and out. He knew both the science and how to communicate and share his passion for meteorology to a wider audience.

Whilst I did not know Alan personally, I was all too aware of his work. Despite my being a professional meteorologist for more than 35 years, to this day I describe myself as an 'enthusiastic amateur'. You might ask if with a PhD in meteorology, and as a lecturer to the next generation of forecaster at the University of Birmingham, as well as being the founder and owner of meteorological companies, I have gone past the stage of being an 'amateur'.

But that label is not one to be used to suggest inferior knowledge of a subject, rather one to extol that a subject is not just a profession but a way of life. From Alan's writing it is clear that he too was an 'enthusiastic amateur' and it is an honour to be in such company.

Whilst gaining knowledge of meteorology during more youthful times, I avidly digested *Instant Weather Forecasting*, hanging on Alan's every word and using his words as my guide when looking up to the skies and predicting the weather of the coming hours.

In Alan's preface to the fifth edition of *Instant Weather Forecasting* he estimated that over half a million copies of the book have been sold worldwide; a total which has now been surpassed. This shows the faith that readers have in the book, and as so often with such publications it is recommendations made by others which ensures the book continues to be useful to the next generation.

And so it was with some trepidation that I agreed to undertake the task of updating *Instant Weather Forecasting*. In doing so I have tried to stay true to Alan's ethos which comes through so strongly in his book. There are updates to pictures and diagrams, bringing them up to date and making them easier to understand. However, I am hopeful that the book remains an invaluable guide to the skies and the weather of the hours ahead, as Alan intended when he wrote the first edition during the hot summer of 1967.

Simon Keeling

How to use this book

When the sky has a certain look it is very often followed by a certain sequence of weather events. There are red skies, blue skies, thundery skies, but how can one be sure that the weather forecast that the clouds are foretelling will turn out to be correct? Many of us will have seen that threatening, thundery sky pass by without a drop of rain. A red sky at night, despite the warning, can sometimes precede a fine day.

In the twenty-four cloud studies shown in this book, there is only room for the clearest inferences and sometimes the weather will not develop as expected. Even so, on perhaps 75 per cent of occasions, the pictures in this book and the short notes which go with them will prove to be largely correct in foretelling the coming hours.

So, here's how to get the most from this book:

1. Find the sky which most resembles the one you have.

2. See if the Major Clues are there as well. If they are, that's your cue to read the Major Inference and the Explanation which accompanies each study.

3. If the sky still seems to fit the present situation, consult the meteorological elements of greatest interest to you (say, Wind and Precipitation) to find the most likely trend and the normal period over which it will occur.

Timing errors tend to be the most frequent aspects to let down a forecast, so if bad weather is expected then it is better to assume it will come sooner than expected rather than later, especially if at sea.

To call any book on weather *Instant Forecasting* is, if taken literally, likely to give the impression that the road to becoming a forecaster of your own weather is easy and quick. This is not so. There are many years of experience in this book but others without professional forecasting experience have used the ideas put forward here and have found that they work. I hope they work for you.

When conditions are generally described without qualification they tend to refer specifically to the temperate latitudes of the Northern Hemisphere.

If you are in the Southern Hemisphere the rules need to be changed and you can find out how on page 7. In general, a wind veer (that is moving clockwise, ie from 6 to 9 on the clock face) quoted in the text should be read as the wind backing (moving anticlockwise, ie from 6 to 3) in the Southern Hemisphere.

The message of the high clouds and the other phenomena from which short-term forecasts may be made are the same regardless of where the observer happens to be.

However, it is important to note that in the lee of mountains or in the middle of continents or the ocean there can be wide divergences from some of the conditions described in this book.

The temperature indications are based on 'sensation value' ie what it feels like rather than just the actual air temperature. This is because wind speed is often of major importance in cooling the body and in so doing offsets the effects of high air temperature. Alternatively, a calm, clear winter's day may become bitterly cold without any change of air temperature just because the wind gets up.

As most people wish to forecast the weather for recreation and holidays, the major inferences given are generally for those months of spring, summer and autumn when the weather is fit for outdoor activity.

A gap in the brief statements of the likely trends and changes merely indicates that nothing of great use can be said under these headings. It does not indicate that there will be no changes at all, but that any changes that do occur will be relatively minor.

The Crossed Winds Rules

Changeable, and often unpleasant, weather comes about when a succession of lows (or depressions) passes over any locality. Surface winds tend to back (move anti-clockwise) when poorer weather is coming and to veer (move clockwise) when better weather is on the way.

These are, however, rather vague rules. If we get a little more clever with the winds that we observe both at the surface, and the way in which the clouds are moving, our forecasts can improve. The Cross Winds Rule helps us with this. There are three of these rules.

Figure 1 can seem rather daunting at first. However, it simply shows the winds flowing around an area of low pressure. The blue lines denote the wind direction at lower levels. The red lines denote the winds at cloud level (at whatever level you can best observe them from the ground). The closer together the lines, the stronger the winds. Notice how they are flowing around the area of low pressure.

Lower and upper winds are not independent of one another – the way they flow across or parallel to one another is governed by the temperature of the next major air mass which is coming along.

In the diagram you can see a block of warm air in the warm sector (the air between the warm and the cold front, shaded in red). At point A, where the warm air mass of the depression is going to arrive later, the surface wind (blue line) is crossed at right angles with the upper wind (red line).

Now look behind the cold front. See how the winds are equally crossed at right angles, but in the opposite sense, where a mass of cold air follows behind the front. The weather will eventually change from blustery showers to fair weather.

So, at (A) the weather is going to deteriorate, while at (C) it is going to improve. Thus we arrive at the following rules which we will be calling the Crossed Winds Rules. These are (in the Northern Hemisphere):

1. Stand with your back to the lower wind and if upper winds (or clouds) come from the left hand then the weather will normally deteriorate.

2. Stand with your back to the lower wind and if upper winds (or clouds) come from the right hand the weather will normally improve.

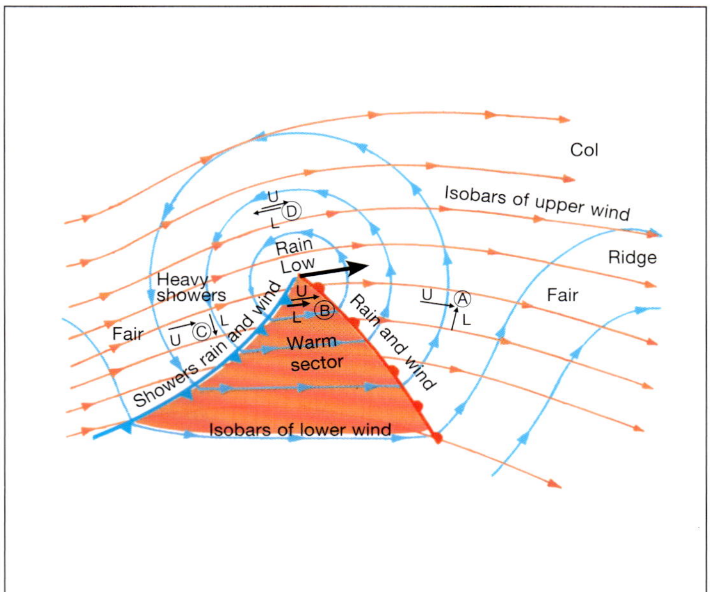

Fig 1 To illustrate the Crossed Winds Rules.

In the Southern Hemisphere temperate latitudes, if you stand with your face to the lower wind the same rules apply.

Strictly speaking, the lower wind is not the surface wind, although it will be on most occasions. Ideally the lower wind direction is the direction of motion clouds such as cumulus, stratocumulus or other low clouds.

The third part of the rules is illustrated at (B) and (D) in Fig 1. Here the air masses are, in fact, all the same air mass from top to bottom of the troposphere and the upper and lower winds are flowing either parallel in the same direction or parallel in opposite directions. This means that no major front is in the immediate offing and so we can say:

3. Stand with your back to the lower wind and if upper winds (or clouds) move on a parallel course the weather will normally not change very much for a while.

Hints on recognising the direction and speed of the upper wind from the clouds are given in the descriptions accompanying the photographs, which have, in many cases, been chosen to help in using the rules for forecasting.

Note that the rules are good for forecasting the weather of the next few hours, not a day in advance (although they may help). Much depends on the sky and the speed of movement of weather systems.

This description of the Crossed Winds Rules does not purport to be complete in every aspect, but it is ample for the purposes of this book, although readers who want to know more should look at *The Weather Handbook*, also by Alan Watts.

Explanation of terms used in the text

The numbers below refer to the skies depicted in the book.

Air Masses come from semi-permanent source regions which are large anticyclones. The following are those of the North Atlantic area.

Name	Abbreviation	Typical weather	Source
Maritime Tropical	mT	Extensively cloudy with rain and drizzle. Poor visibility and fog. 9, 10, 22	Azores High
Maritime Polar	mP	Showers and bright periods. Good visibility. 11, 12, 13, 15, 24	Polar High
Returning Maritime Polar	rmP	Cool but fair. Good visibility. 19, 21	As mP but modified by Atlantic Ocean
Continental Polar	cP	Intensely cold and often cloudy in winter	Siberian High
Continental Tropical	cT	Very warm and often cloudless. 7, 17	Southern Europe or North Africa

Anticyclone or High A region of mainly subsiding air with outflowing winds and often clearing skies. Sometimes, especially in winter, anticyclones are totally overcast for days on end.

Castellanus is normally lines of altostratus cloud out of which grow turrets of cumuliform clouds. It is a cloud which presages thundery outbreaks some hours hence. See 7 and 17.

Cloud Cover is measured in eighths of the sky covered. In our usage it will tend to mean the cover which is likely to affect the area from where the observations are made. For example, a western sky full of cirrus and altostratus from an advancing front will constitute half cover, ie, four-eighths or so, but nondescript clouds on the horizon of an otherwise clear sky and which are obviously not advancing over-rapidly need not be counted as cloud cover at all.

Cloudy A cloudy sky is one where the total cloud wholly covers or nearly covers the entire sky.

Col The slack pressure region between two highs or two lows.

Cold Front The zone of division between a warm air mass (usually tropical maritime) and a cold one (usually Polar maritime). Cold fronts tend to pass in half the time that warm fronts take to pass. The cold frontal surface slopes backwards and has about twice the slope of the warm front. (Fig 2, page 10).

Cyclonic Winds vary cyclonically if they change progressively in accordance with the way that is expected when a depression (or cyclone) moves across the observer. Winds which are cyclonic move progressively clockwise as a low centre moves to the north of the observer in the Northern Hemisphere but they move anti-clockwise when it passes to the south.

Depression or Low A region of mainly ascending air accompanied by precipitation and strong winds. A low is a bad weather system; old lows though, without fronts, may not bring very bad weather.

Diurnal Variation Air temperature near the earth's surface is at a maximum soon after midday (sun time) and at a minimum soon after dawn. The change from maximum to minimum and back again is called diurnal variation of temperature. Wind speed and cumulus cloud cover follows the same diurnal variation, being at its maximum in the early afternoon and at its minimum around dawn. Humidity is exactly opposite, being lowest in the afternoon and highest around dawn.

Fallstreaks are 'showers' of ice from high clouds — usually cirrus — which sink through many thousands of feet of the upper atmosphere. As they sink they become deflected by falling into wind at lower levels which is normally less strong than that above when ahead of bad weather systems. They, thus, appear to trail backwards from the heads of the parent cloud from which they originate. Because of the interrelation of winds and temperatures of air masses the general direction in which the tails of the streaks point is towards a warm air mass. Thus, fallstreaks ahead of warm fronts often point to the SW, and those behind cold fronts point to the SE. (NW and NE, respectively, in the Southern Hemisphere.)

Dense streaks combined with a very strong drop in wind speed as they fall produce the jet stream banners of **1**. They produce streaks in one general direction ahead of less strong bad weather systems as in **2** and **3**, and behind such systems as described in **16**. They are dense, twisted and much more vertical ahead of thundery troughs in summer. When they sink in several directions they mean that good weather will persist. If they stream out parallel to the surface wind then they indicate no immediate change, as in **20**.

Fine and Fair In this book the term fine means that the skies are mainly clear, with less than two to three-eighths cloud cover, while fair means a partly cloudy sky with between three and six-eighths cloud cover. In either case there is no precipitation. At night the word clear has the same meaning as fine.

Floccus A form of altocumulus cloud associated with thundery weather, which resembles a flock of woolly sheep. Often seen with castellanus.

Fog may come from radiation cooling the ground as in **14**, by being moved in on the back of a wind (advection fog) as in **10** or when a warm wind arrives over cold ground, as during a rapid thaw. Risk of radiation fog increases with the night in quiet conditions, and is aided by industrial and domestic smoke. Places downwind or downhill from built-up areas are particularly prone. Radiation fogs normally disperse with the sun, but encroachment of cloud may cut off the sun and make for a persistent fog. If in winter this cloud is stratocumulus then smog may form.

Advection fogs come in ahead of encroaching fronts and also when sea breezes start to blow on spring and early summer days. Increase of wind sometimes lifts fog into low stratus cloud.

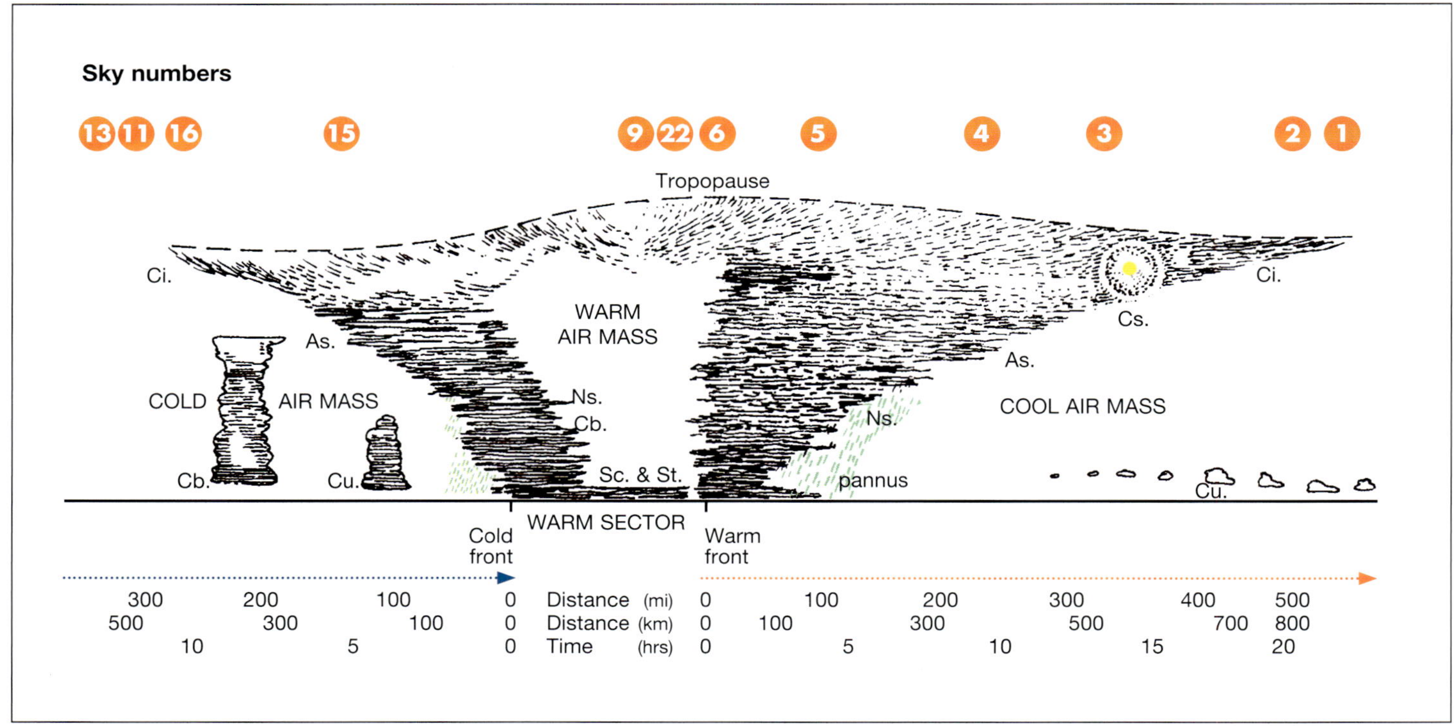

Fig 2 Cross-section through the front of a developed depression. The distances and times are typical ones and are given for clouds and weather ahead of the warm front and behind the cold front. The warm sector may last for many hours or may be entirely absent. In the latter case the depression is occluding. The resultant occluded front is then formed by moving the cold and warm fronts into coincidence. Figures in orange above the diagram show where the skies with these numbers might be seen.

Fractus is a form of stratus and is associated with the ragged fragments seen when this low cloud is forming or dispersing.

Frost needs cool air and clear skies. It will form first in hollows and low-lying areas protected from the wind. The ground will fall below freezing first (ground frost). If the cooling continues it will extend slowly into the air deck above the cold ground (air frost). If a frost occurs with a moderate wind then this is likely to be a severe frost.

Inversions The air temperature normally falls with height at an average 'lapse rate' of 4.5°F per 1,000 ft of ascent (8°C per km). When, as at night in quiet conditions, the earth cools, then the air over it cools, leaving warmer strata above. Then the lapse rate is reversed and temperature increases for a certain distance with height. This deck of air where the lapse rate is reversed is called an inversion. Very strong inversions occur when air subsides from higher levels and warms up. The tropopause is a strong and permanent inversion which seals all the weather processes below it. Inversions at any height tend to do the same. They trap layer clouds like stratocumulus and altostratus.

Jet Streams High speed rivers of wind snaking round the temperate and sub-tropical latitudes of both Hemispheres. They are normally at about 30,000 ft (10 km) and are associated with the formation and movement of depressions. Characteristic clouds 1 form with them and so help to foretell the coming bad weather. Unseasonal weather occurs when the jets move from their normal latitudes.

Knot A speed of one nautical mile per hour. The normal unit for wind speed throughout the world. 1 kt = 1.15 mph = 1.855 km per hr.

Nebulosis is the form of stratus associated with total cover at a very low level 22.

Occluded Front Cold fronts move faster than warm ones so that eventually a cold front overtakes a warm one and the warm air becomes progressively lifted from the surface. In Fig 3 (page 13) this process has already started in the low near New York and it is on the point of starting in the low over the Faeroes. The zone of division between cool air ahead and cold air behind is called a cold occlusion. If the air behind the front is warmer than ahead it is a warm occlusion. Most land areas experience more occlusions than other types of front.

Orographic Rain Rain formed by the lifting of a moist airstream over hills. Over mountains the precipitation may be snow or sleet at any time of year. Airstreams which produce no precipitation over open country or coastal plains may well produce heavy and continuous rain, showers, thunderstorms etc when forced to traverse hill ridges.

Pannus is a form of stratus which is caused by turbulent wind eddies lifting and cooling the airspace below a cloud base from which rain, snow or sleet is falling. The latter will not necessarily reach the ground, as it evaporates as it falls and so moistens the airspace. Pannus foretells immediate rain, but once it has begun to rain in earnest it may extend into total cover at 1,000 ft (300 m) or so. See 5.

Pressure Tendency The fall of pressure with time (ie, tendency) is taken here to mean the following:

Major fall (or rise)	8–10 millibars or more in 3 hours
Rapid fall (or rise)	6–8 mb/3 hrs
Moderate fall (or rise)	between 3 and 6 mb/3 hrs
Slow fall (or rise)	less than 3 mb/3 hrs

The tendency is taken over 3 hours to allow time for a trend to reveal itself as a real one and not just a temporary small change. (Note that in some countries the pressure unit of hectopascal hP is used, however the hP is exactly the same change of pressure as the millibar.)

Ridge of High Pressure A region, usually the extension of a high where air is subsiding. See Fig 1.

Seabreezes Local winds that blow onto coasts during the days of spring and summer. They need light morning wind and sunshine, may penetrate tens of miles inland, and may draw their air from just as far seaward.

Seabreeze front When light winds from the land try to oppose seabreezes, a line like a miniature cold front develops between the two winds. Here the winds change from blowing off the land to blowing on to it.

Explanation of terms used in the text

Showers grow in unstable airstreams which are moist (eg Polar maritime air). There may be little diurnal variation over the sea or on windward facing coasts, but inland showers rarely spread themselves evenly over the day. Hill slopes force showery airstreams to disgorge their moisture as rain or snow and so shower-free areas may exist in the lee of hills and mountain ranges. Inland, mornings that are clear and cool may break out into showers by the late morning or early afternoon 11. Air mass troughs 12 often reserve most of the showers for themselves. Nights are clear inland away from the windward coasts and stars are very bright.

Stable Airstream An airstream is stable if air which is forced to ascend in it, either by thermals or by being lifted over hills or frontal surfaces, tends to sink back again. An airstream may have stable layers over unstable ones or vice versa. A temperature inversion separates a lower, unstable layer from a stable one higher up. The signs of stable airstreams are layer clouds, sinking funnel or chimney smoke which tends to hang together and is not easily dispersed, poor visibility and extremes of temperature. Airstreams which are warmer than the surface over which they travel are stable near the surface.

Stratosphere The region of the upper atmosphere above the tropopause. No weather processes of any significance occur there.

Summer Half of the Year That period of the year which comprises the warmest and sunniest months with least cold weather and fewest major storms.

Thunderstorms may be single (air mass thunderstorm) 13, in lines (frontal thunderstorms) 8, or in areas often associated with slack pressure (col). A single storm is a cell of rising and sinking air currents with an active lifetime of 20 minutes to half an hour. When aided by frontal ascent (particularly cold fronts) then downdraughts due to rain and hail produce cold 'whalebacks' of air around a cell and lift the air there into new cells. These daughter cells take over from the dying parent. Medium-level storms have their bases some 6,000–10,000 ft (2,000–3,000 m) aloft and may follow the skies shown in 7 and 17, depending on the winds aloft and below.

Thundery Rain follows the appearance of chaotic streaks, dapples, lines and waves in the build-up of the medium cloud ahead of a front. It is heavy here and there but thunder does not necessarily occur – just thunder-type spots.

Thundery Sky has cloud elements arranged in lines but the different directions of alignment at different levels give the appearance of chaos. It need not be entirely associated with the summer half of the year. The Crossed Winds Rules can be used to differentiate the forecast of 7 from that of 17.

Trails formed by aircraft help to tell wind speed and direction aloft. When they are dense they indicate the possible incidence of a warm front. When they do not persist they indicate a relatively dry upper atmosphere and therefore little chance of major deterioration. High speed upper winds shred trails rapidly. If they shred sideways then the wind is across the trails, as in 3. If they form castellated tops then the wind is parallel to the trails.

Tropopause The region of the atmosphere above about 8 miles (13 km) up which puts a 'lid' on weather processes by preventing any further ascent of air from the troposphere. It is characterised by temperature remaining constant with height.

Troposphere The region of the atmosphere in which weather processes occur. It is characterised by the temperature falling off with height, a situation which is arrested by the tropopause (see *Unstable Airstream* and *Inversions*).

Trough A region, often the extension of a low, where air is mainly ascending, leading to rain, showers etc, and temporary deterioration. There are two types of trough **1.** frontal and **2.** air mass. The former owes its existence to a front (usually an old one), while the latter forms in unstable Polar airstreams especially in the rear of depressions.

Unstable Airstream An airstream in which ascending air continues to do so for a considerable depth of the atmosphere. An inversion will eventually stop the ascent and cut off the clouds at a certain upper level. The highest (and most impenetrable) level that clouds can reach is the tropopause. Cirrus and cumulonimbus must both have their tops below the tropopause which is about 8 miles (13 km) aloft over temperate latitudes of either Hemisphere. It is about 5 miles (8 km) aloft over the Poles and 10 miles (16 km) up over the Equator. Unstable airstreams are characterised by cumuliform clouds, lifting and dispersing smoke, good visibility and moderate temperature.

Veering and Backing The wind is said to veer when it changes direction clockwise and to back when it changes direction anti-clockwise.

Virga is trailing wisps of low cloud seen under the lowest parts of active fronts as they are passing. It may nearly reach the ground, especially when it snows.

Warm Front The zone of division between a cool or cold air mass and a warm one. The representative air masses are maritime Polar ahead of the front (often warmed up and stabilised by time) and tropical maritime air behind.

The warm front is where a warm frontal surface meets the earth's surface, and the air behind the front gives its name to the front.

Warm Sector The block of tropical maritime air enclosed by the warm and cold fronts of a depression (Fig 3).

Winter Half of the Year That period of the year in any latitude which comprises the worst months, ie coldest and windiest with most major storms. It need not coincide with the official dates of winter and can extend from autumn through to spring.

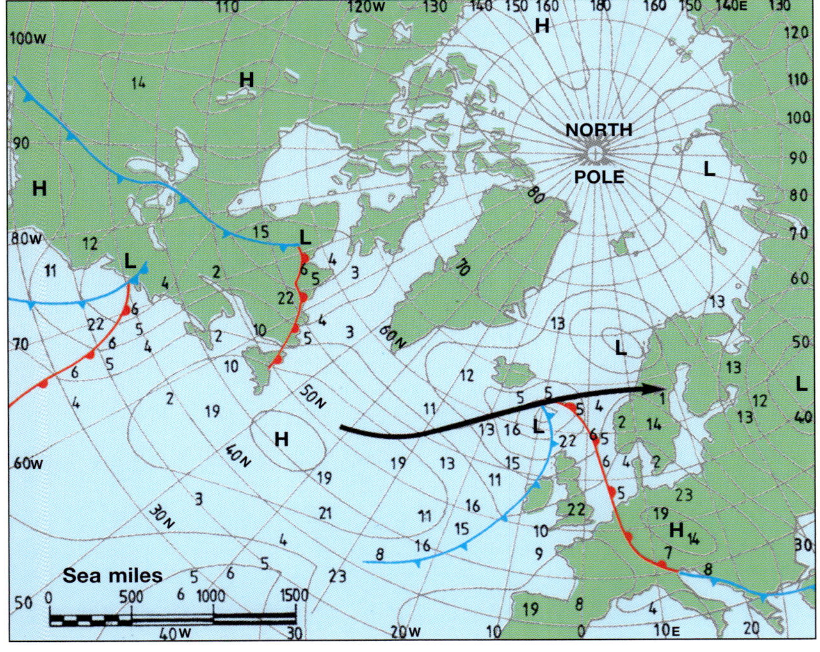

Fig 3 This actual weather map of part of the Northern Hemisphere illustrates possible places where the skies **1** to **24** might be seen. The thick black arrow is a jet stream. It is only part of the total jet which will snake more-or-less continuously round the temperate latitudes. Jet stream cirrus, depicted as appearing at the head of the jet **1** may be seen anywhere just to the south of the jet but is often obscured by the cloud of the depression. Cross-section through the fronts of a depression in Fig 2 could be either along say 55°N spanning Britain, or along 35°N across the warm sector of the depression centred round New York.

Facts about clouds

Clouds can be divided into three height decks:

1. The region of low clouds
 – cloud bases between land surface and 7,000 ft (0–2 km).

2. The region of medium clouds
 – cloud bases between 7,000 and 25,000 ft (2–8 km).

3. The region of high clouds
 – cloud bases between 16,000 and 45,000 ft (5–13 km).

These divisions are generally applicable, but medium and high clouds sink below their lower limits in winter and with increasing latitude. In the tropics all clouds tend to rise above the upper limits for their type. Thus the divisions are only a guide. The best indication is the cloud type, eg cirrus is a higher cloud than altostratus, and altostratus higher than cumulus, etc.

Clouds are further classified by shape:

a Heap clouds (cumuliform)
b Layer clouds (stratiform)
c Feathery clouds (cirriform)

Having established the general cloud divisions the following table gives the major types. Height and shape numbers refer to the divisions given above.

Height and shape	Name	Abbreviation	Description
1a	Cumulus	Cu	Low heap clouds of small vertical extent
1ab	Stratocumulus	Sc	Low heap-layer clouds either broken or covering the whole sky
123a	Cumulonimbus	Cb	Heap clouds of great vertical extent producing showers and thunderstorms
1b	Stratus	St	Low, or very low, amorphous layer clouds covering coasts and hills
123b	Nimbostratus	Ns	Layered – often solid – clouds of great vertical extent associated with bad weather
2ab	Altocumulus	Ac	Medium level heap clouds in 'islands' or 'rafts' seldom covering the whole sky. The normal form is often associated with the term 'mackerel sky' but other forms are lenticularis (lens-shaped) and castellanus and floccus (chaotic clouds of thundery skies)
2b	Altostratus	As	Medium level layer clouds associated with the term 'a watery sun'
3c	Cirrus	Ci	High clouds mainly formed by more-or-less dense heads from which fall streaks or trails (fallstreaks) so producing hooks, banners, etc. Associated with the term 'mares' tails'
3ab	Cirrocumulus	Cc	High heap clouds ranged together in sheets of dappled, rippled etc. appearance. Also associated with the term 'mackerel sky'
3b	Cirrostratus	Cs	High amorphous cloud often covering the entire sky and sometimes only revealed by the presence of haloes about sun or moon.

Beaufort Scale of wind force

Beaufort number	General description	Sea criterion	Landsman's criterion	Velocity in knots
0	Calm	Sea like a mirror	Calm. Smoke rises vertically	Less than 1
1	Light air	Ripples with the appearance of scales are formed but without foam crests	Direction of wind shown by smoke drift but not by wind vanes	1 to 3
2	Light breeze	Small wavelets, still short but more pronounced. Crests have a glassy appearance and do not break	Wind felt on face. Leaves rustle. Ordinary vane moved by wind	4 to 6
3	Gentle breeze	Large wavelets. Crests begin to break. Foam of glassy appearance. Perhaps scattered white horses	Leaves and small twigs in constant motion. Wind extends light flags	7 to 10
4	Moderate breeze	Small waves becoming longer. Fairly frequent white horses	Raises dust and loose paper. Small branches are moved	11 to 16
5	Fresh breeze	Moderate waves, taking a more pronounced long form. Many white horses are formed. Chance of some spray	Small trees in leaf begin to sway. Crested wavelets form on inland waters	17 to 21
6	Strong breeze	Large waves begin to form. The white foam crests are more extensive everywhere. Probably some spray	Large branches in motion. Whistling in telegraph wires. Umbrellas used with difficulty	22 to 27
7	Near gale	Sea heaps up and white foam from breaking waves begins to be blown in streaks along the direction of the wind	Whole trees in motion. Inconvenience felt when walking against the wind	28 to 33
8	Gale	Moderately high waves of greater length. Edges of crests begin to break into spindrift. The foam is blown in well-marked streaks along the direction of the wind	Breaks twigs off trees. Generally impedes progress	34 to 40
9	Strong gale	High waves. Dense streaks of foam along the direction of the wind. Crests of waves begin to topple, tumble and roll over. Spray may affect visibility	Slight structural damage occurs (chimney pots and slates removed)	41 to 47
10	Storm	Very high waves with long overhanging crests. Foam in great patches is blown in dense white streaks along the direction of the wind. The surface takes on a white appearance. The tumbling of the sea becomes heavy and shock-like. Visibility affected	Seldom experienced inland. Trees uprooted. Considerable structural damage occurs	48 to 55

Jet stream cirrus

MAJOR INFERENCE A vigorous cyclonic situation exists upwind and so gales may occur within the next 8–15 hours.

MAJOR CLUES **1**. Long parallel banners formed by cirrus cloud heads showering ice crystals into slower wind below these clouds. When strongly developed, the fallstreaks combine into bands of cloud stretched along the direction of the upper winds. This flow is usually from west to east or north-west to south-east (as in the photograph). (South-west to north-east in the Southern Hemisphere.) **2**. Cirrus elements actually seen to move across the sky are usually going at over 80 knots (94 mph) and marked movement indicates real jet stream speeds of 100–160 kt so changes in the weather are usually fast.

EXPLANATION Jet streams play a major role in the formation of vigorous surface depressions. These develop some hundreds of miles away on the equatorial side of the jet stream. Cirrus clouds do the same and, thus, the latter show that a vigorous depression may well be forming and moving into the area soon. But as the banners are dense when fully formed, they take some time to disperse and so can outlive the growth phase of the depression with which they formed. However, the Crossed Winds Rules will help in assessing the likelihood of real deterioration. In the picture the aircraft trail which is spreading sideways in the direction of the banners further confirms that the wind up there is from bottom right and spreading towards the reader.

Element	Trend	Normal change	Normally in	Risk of	Possibly
Wind	Increase and back into southern quadrants	Force 2–4 W to NW becoming Force 5–8 SW to SE	6–12 hours	Force 6 in 3–6 hours	Severe gale or storm later, esp at sea in winter half of the year
Visibility	Good or exceptional then decrease	30 miles or more at first, decreasing to 10 miles or less	10–15 hours	Sea and hill fog by end of period	
Precipitation	Rain or snow	Continuous, moderate later	10–15 hours	Heavy rain or snow later	Light or intermittent if situation does not develop
Cloud	2–4/8 Ci, increasing from west	8/8 Cs, then 8/8 As, 8/8 Ns, Sc and pannus when real deterioration	10–15 hours	6–8/8 Sc forming to obscure upper cloud build-up	3–6/8 high and medium cloud if situation does not develop
Temperature	Becoming cooler	Feels cooler as sun is cut off and wind increases	5–10 hours	Bitter in winter	Little change if wind does not develop
Pressure	Falling	Moderate fall under Ci but speeding up. Rapid fall leads to Force 6–8 but major fall may give Force 9–10 at sea	12–24 hours	Major fall and more rapid (halve the times) passage of depression	Slow fall and so longer build-up of wind etc

Cirrus and cirrostratus

MAJOR INFERENCE The warm front of a depression is probably on the way, so the wind will increase and rain is likely later – or snow in winter.

MAJOR CLUES 1. Cirrus skies do not often look as organised as in we see in 1 *Jet stream cirrus*, but if the cirrus filaments mostly stream in the same direction, the weather may deteriorate rapidly. **2.** The Crossed Winds Rule for deterioration should be evident (surface wind blowing into the back of the observer while the Ci streams in from their left-hand side) showing that a warmer air mass is on the way, ie there is a warm front or occlusion approaching (for *left* read *right* in the Southern Hemisphere.) **3**. Good visibility (and heap clouds if present) show that you have a colder, Polar air mass overhead and a temperature contrast with warm air to come, a combination that often creates an active front. **4**. The appearance of a halo ring, as shown in the picture opposite, shows that you now have the second in the sequence of clouds preceding an active warm front – cirrostratus – so it is more likely that wind and rain will follow.

EXPLANATION The model depression (Fig 2) leads to the expectation of a wedge of relatively warm air, extending hundreds of miles from where the warm front meets the surface. The cirrus of 1 forms in the high, thin, leading edge of the front. As the wedge deepens, the cirrostratus of 2 often covers most of the sky. Its appearance, with a halo following a build-up of cirrus, makes it highly likely that wind and rain will follow. Darker lower layers of altostratus cloud follow, and then, eventually, low rain-bearing nimbostratus. In the Northern Hemisphere, winds to the south of the low pressure centre increase and back (shift anti-clockwise) as the front approaches whilst those to the north of the low winds increase less and veer (shift clockwise). In the Southern Hemisphere for *back* read *veer* and vice versa.

Element	Trend	Normal change	Normally in	Risk of	Possibly
Wind	Backing and increasing	Force 2–4 SW–S, becoming Force 5–7 S–SE	3–8 hours	Force 8–9	Force 4–5 in summer if depression weak
Visibility	Increase then decrease	10–13 miles or more, becoming 2–4 miles in rain, ½–1 mile snow	6–12 hours	Fog by end of period	4–6 miles in light rain
Precipitation	Rain or snow	Continuous slight to continuous moderate	6–12 hours	Heavy rain, thunder in summer half of year	Slight rain if depression weak
Cloud	Increasing to overcast	8/8 Cs then 8/8 As then 8/8 Ns with Sc and pannus	6–12 hours	8/8 low stratus covering coasts and hills	Broken skies if depression weak
Temperature	Cooler	Cooler as wind increases cooler still in pptn.	3–8 hours	Bitter in snow in winter	Little change if depression weak
Pressure	Falling	Moderate fall, followed by rapid fall later	10–20 hours	Major fall later with gales	Slow fall if depression weak

Warm front or occlusion approaching

SKY ASSOCIATED WITH **DETERIORATION**

MAJOR INFERENCE Moderate deterioration.

MAJOR CLUES **1**. Upper cloud (cirrus) and medium level cloud (altostratus) approaching. **2**. Upper winds are strong and across the trails made by the cloud as the altostratus are being rapidly shredded. **3**. Lowest cloud (altostratus) aligned to show that upper cloud and wind is coming from the left of the lower (ie from bottom left to upper right).

EXPLANATION The sky has the hallmarks of a warm front approaching, but there are breaks in the cloud build-up. This indicates an older and possibly less virile system than the skies in **1** and **2**. Features in the As on the horizon are aligned in the same direction as those of the cirrus at the top of the picture. This means that the wind at As level is perpendicular to that at Ci level because Ci features stream with the wind, while As features lay across the wind (as with many clouds of a stable type). Thus, the sky is set for deterioration but the breaks indicate a moderate and possible slow change to more wind and rain.

Element	Trend	Normal change	Normally in	Risk of	Possibly
Wind	Moderate increase and back	Force 5–6 SW to SE	6–12 hours	Force 6–7	Cyclonic Force 2–5
Visibility	Decrease later	2–4 miles in rain, ½–1 mile in snow	6–12 hours	½ mile in heavy rain 100 yards in snow	Fog over high ground later
Precipitation	Rain or snow	Continuous moderate	6–12 hours	Heavy rain over hills	Drizzle later
Cloud	Increase	8/8 As and Ns	3–6 hours	8/8 low St later	Broken cloud later
Temperature	Cooler	Cooler due to increase of wind	Next few hours	Cold in winter	Hot later in summer
Pressure	Falling	Moderate fall but if rapid go for stronger wind	8–12 hours	Rapid fall for gale	Slow fall for Force 2–3

Altostratus ahead of a warm front or occlusion

MAJOR INFERENCE If this sky follows that in 1 with cirrostratus (haloes) between, then expect a major deterioration. If it follows 2 and some cirrostratus then expect a deterioration too. If following 3 often without cirrostratus and with substantial breaks in the cloud build-up, expect a moderate deterioration

MAJOR CLUES **1**. Organised flat and often featureless grey cloud through which the sun gradually recedes as if disappearing behind ground glass. **2**. Should have been preceded by Ci and Cs, but any cumulus will shred and die away as the sun is cut off from the ground. **3**. Lineal features of As lying across the wind of the medium levels show the wind direction there and can be combined with the surface wind so that the Crossed Winds Rules can be applied.

EXPLANATION Altostratus like this when following Ci and Cs is an almost certain prognosis of rain and wind increase. Fragments of dark cloud which appear below the much higher altostratus layer can be the remains of cumulus and may indicate immediate rain or snow (see page 24). These will soon disappear as high cloud thickens. Steady thickening, lack of major features and muddy greyness all contribute to a forecast of a fairly immediate deterioration. Winds should be backing into the southern quadrant of the compass and increasing when we are to the south of an advancing area of low pressure (for Southern Hemisphere see the note on page 7).

Element	Trend	Normal change	Normally in	Risk of	Possibly
Wind	Rapid increase and back	Force 6–7 in winter, Force 5–6 in summer	4–6 hours	Force 8–10	Cyclonic force 4–6 if shallow depression
Visibility	Increase then decrease	Tens of miles, then 2–4 miles in precipitation	2–4 hours	½ mile in snow (or less)	Generally good
Precipitation	Rain or snow	Continuous moderate	2–4 hours	Heavy rain or snow	Intermittent, slight pptn.
Cloud	Increase and lowering	8/8 Ns with pannus 5 and virga 6	2–4 hours	Fog over hills and at sea	Broken Sc and St later
Temperature	Cooler	Cooler due to wind increase and no sun	Next hour or two	Very cold in winter	Warmer later if cloud breaks
Pressure	Falling	Moderate or rapid fall	4–6 hours	Major fall for severe gale	Slow fall if shallow depression

Imminent rain or snow

MAJOR INFERENCE Rain or snow will commence very shortly and sometimes almost immediately.

MAJOR CLUES **1**. A totally overcast and lowering sky coupled with – **2**. Ragged, developing lumps of grey cloud coming from the direction of the wind (windward) below the main cloudbase. The cloud lumps forming below the higher altostratus layer are called pannus. The formation of pannus indicates that it is already at cloud level, although the little rain drops will not survive to the ground – yet! However, pannus is a sure sign that rain is imminent.

EXPLANATION This sky tells you to reach for the umbrella! These are all the signs of an approaching warm front. The sun has long since disappeared behind the grey featureless altostratus. The camera in this picture was looking into the south and the pannus is forming in the wet air below the base of the As and streaming in on the lower wind.

Element	Trend	Normal change	Normally in	Risk of	Possibly
Wind	Increase	Increase by 1–2 Beaufort Forces	A few minutes	Gusts	Little change
Visibility	Decrease	Lower by a few miles in rain to less than 1 mile in snow	Half an hour or an hour	Fog limits in snow	Little change
Precipitation	Immediate commencement	Intermittent at first, becoming continuous moderate	A few minutes		Wholly intermittent
Cloud	To total cover of pannus	6–8/8 pannus or Sc and St below 8/8 As and Ns	An hour or two	Covering hills	3–5/8 pannus or Sc
Temperature	Immediate fall	Cooler in downdraughts caused by falling rain	Tens of minutes	Suddenly very cold in winter	Little immediate change if rain slight
Pressure	Continuing fall	Moderate or rapid fall	2–6 hours	Major fall	Slow fall if shallow depression

A front passes

MAJOR INFERENCE Change imminent. In bad weather the break is often not as marked as shown in the photograph. It may just be a lightening of the sky behind a trailing cloud base. Expect gusts and a veering wind, a steadying of or a rise in pressure, a change of air mass and change of humidity and air temperature, and a change in intensity of precipitation or its type, ie rain to drizzle, rain to showers etc.

MAJOR CLUES **1**. This is a warm front when total low cloud cover and cool rain changes to a higher cloud base and rain stops. Lower cloud may, however, soon close in again with high humidity and drizzle. **2**. This is a cold front when warm, humid tropical air changes to cool, moist Polar air and visibility becomes good. There is a period of rain and showers. Cumulus cloud can be seen on the windward horizon. **3**. This is an occluded front when the warm front is followed by the cold front without any tropical air mass between them.

EXPLANATION A photograph of a weak warm front passing was chosen because more virile fronts show few contrasts in their features. However, the trends are illustrated. There is a low cloud line with trailing virga hanging beneath the cloud. Beyond this the sky is brighter and so there is an obvious change of weather type. Rain now falling can be expected to cease as the lowest cloud passes.

Element	Trend	Normal change	Normally in	Risk of	Possibly
Wind	Immediate veer, gusty	Veer behind lowest cloud with wind increase	Tens of minutes	Heavy gusts from left hand of present wind	Wind decrease or little change of direction
Visibility	Decrease	Decrease as front passes. Poor behind warm front. Increase behind cold front	Tens of minutes	Fog behind warm front	Little change when front weak
Precipitation	Immediate cessation of continuous moderate rain	Very low cloud and drizzle when a warm front. Showers after a time behind cold front	Tens of minutes to an hour or two	Heavy as front clears	None if front weak
Cloud	Lowering, lifting, then lowering again	8/8 Sc and St if warm front, 4/8–6/8 Cu of Cb behind cold front	Half an hour or hour	8/8 low stratus behind warm front	Broken skies with Sc when front weak
Temperature	Warmer if warm front. Cooler if cold front	Muggy due to increased humidity and air mass change when warm front. Fresher when cold front	Tens of minutes		Hot in summer under broken skies
Pressure	Falling, then steady or rising	Steady off if warm front. Rise if cold front	Half an hour or hour	Further fall behind warm front if depression vigorous. Sharp rise behind cold front	Little change with weak fronts

Thundery sky

MAJOR INFERENCE Thundery outbreaks within the next 12 hours or less. Use of the Crossed Winds Rules will tell if an unstable warm front is downwind and so warn of thunderstorms. However, see 17.

MAJOR CLUES **1**. Undulating lines of altocumulus castellanus (looking like turrets of a castle), accompanied by generally disorganised groups of altocumulus floccus with filaments, streaks or small dapples of cloud showing dark against higher clouds. **2**. The weather generally 'feeling' as it does when preceding thundery weather; high temperatures, little wind, possibly high humidity.

EXPLANATION This is the classic 'thundery sky'. The cloud in the lower centre is altocumulus castellanus, which always indicates instability in the middle layers of the atmosphere and so a strong risk of thunder later. Such skies often occur before midday and are followed by sunny spells in the afternoon that allow the land to heat and so prepare the whole lower atmosphere for thunderstorms by evening. This sky, with the orientation for deterioration given in the Crossed Winds Rules, provides a confident forecast of thundery outbreaks.

Element	Trend	Normal change	Normally in	Risk of	Possibly
Wind	Moderate increase	Force 3–4, highly variable	12 hours	Force 7 gusts. Possibly Force 9 gusts	Tornadoes or waterspouts later
Visibility	Decrease	3–6 miles	12 hours	Fog on coasts	Little change
Precipitation	Heavy showers, lightning and thunder	Intermittent or sporadic heavy rain plus hail or rain showers	6–18 hours	Heavy hail later	Little precipitation
Cloud	Decrease, then increase	6–8/8 chaotic As and Ac with Cb and Fr St	6–18 hours	Heavy frontal thunderstorms	Clearance without major deterioration
Temperature	Very hot, followed by catastrophic fall in thunderstorms	Cooler	6–18 hours		Remaining warm
Pressure	Slow fall	Not very marked fall	6–12 hours	Heavy fall with frontal thunderstorms	Little change

8 Thunderstorm

MAJOR INFERENCE Imminent gusts (up to 40–60 knots at their worst), large drop in temperature, thunder and lightning, hail and heavy rain.

MAJOR CLUES 1. Characteristic anvil tops to the cumulonimbus clouds. **2**. Violent upward motions or rolling motions can often be seen in the nearer cloud arches with curious wave-like clouds arriving just ahead of the increase in wind.

EXPLANATION The vertical extent of the thunder clouds that are threatening is often impossible to ascertain because of the surrounding cloud. This photograph shows rolling cloud ahead of an imminent storm. Note the 'rain curtains' in the lower middle of the photograph.

Element	Trend	Normal change	Normally in	Risk of	Possibly
Wind	Violent increase, direction change	Often goes from 5 kt towards storm to gusty Force 5–6 from storm	Half an hour or less, depending on proximity	Gusts to 40–60 kt	Only Force 3–4, gusty
Visibility	Sudden decrease in rain and hail	½ mile or less in heavy rain or hail	Variable time as rain also occurs intermittently, violently	100 yards or less in heavy hail	
Precipitation	Heavy rain or hail showers, thunder, lightning	Intermittent heavy and light periods of rain or hail	Periods occupying approx 10 minutes light and heavy rain, light in rear of storm	Heavy and large hail in worst storms (rare)	Cloudburst, especially in hilly areas late in the day
Cloud	8/8 Cb and related cloud	Rapid increase and very dark waved and rolled clouds under leading edge	5–10 minutes from cloud edge overhead	Tornadoes or waterspouts	Big Cu and As on edges of main cells
Temperature	Dramatic fall	From hot and oppressive to cold, with wind and rain	A few minutes from leading edge of cloud		Little change if storm is just passing
Pressure	Falling slowly	Minor variations under thunderstorms	A few hours	Rapid fall with worst storms	Rising slowly

Warm sector weather

MAJOR INFERENCE In the winter, low cloud, drizzle and mist predominate, as they will around windward-facing coasts at any time of the year, bringing sea, hill and coastal fog too. In the summer, to the lee of higher ground cloud will break and sunny spells develop. Before there can be a major change of weather type a cold front – or several minor fronts – must pass so expect continuation of the weather pattern associated with tropical maritime airstreams. Keep an eye on the sky for major change coming from windward.

MAJOR CLUES **1**. Predominantly cloudy airstream. **2**. Sometimes poor visibility. **3**. Warmth and humidity (often muggy), some drizzle or orographic (hill) rain.

EXPLANATION Warm sector weather comes in many varieties. It follows passage of a warm front and may last from a few hours up to a few days. Immediately behind a warm front it is normally totally cloudy, drizzly and with fog over hills and coasts. Clouds are most often those of stable air, ie stratus and stratocumulus plus plates of cloud in the medium and high levels. However, with bright conditions in the summer, cumulus clouds can form over land, caused by the heat of the day, or the sea may be warmer than the air and set off heap cumulus clouds. Lens-shaped altocumulus lenticularis forms in the lee of hills, as well as high and medium forms of this cloud shape. Sometimes, especially in summer, warm sectors can be thundery.

Element	Trend	Normal change	Normally	Risk of	Possibly
Wind	Remain as now	Diurnal variation of wind speed		Increase to Force 5–6	Decrease
Visibility	Poor	Fog and low cloud	During overnight hours	50 yards or less, especially in winter	Little change
Precipitation	Drizzle on hills and coast	Dry-out with time	Over a day or so	Rain, thunder etc later	Very humid
Cloud	Cloudy	4–7/8 low cloud with patchy medium and high cloud	Usually most cloudy by night and least in latter part of day	8/8 Stratus at 100 ft or less	No cloud
Temperature	Warm for time of year	Follow diurnal variation	Maximum temperature after lunch. Minimum after dawn	Summer temperatures in the eighties, cool under stratus and in fog	
Pressure	Little change	Fall on approach of cold front	In days or hours	Rapid fall and sudden change of air mass, with thunder	Rising steadily

10 Sea and coastal fog

MAJOR INFERENCE Fog banks form over the sea when there is a tropical maritime airstream. In any case the air is warmer than the sea over which it finds itself. Often quite unpredictable in occurrence and extent. Clears as quickly as it arrives. Warning of sea fog sometimes comes from hearing fog signals at sea. In spring and summer, seabreezes may bring it in over beaches. A hot day inland may find coastal resorts wreathed in cold, clammy fog. Also presages formation of low stratus over land and sea at night.

MAJOR CLUES **1**. Warm and humid airstream probably warmer than the sea. **2**. Wind or seabreeze to bring fog in off the sea. **3**. Fog signals heard at sea.

EXPLANATION The coast is often a zone of transition for foggy conditions. Warm, moist onshore winds bring in the fog which soon disperses as it arrives over warm land areas. Shallow sea fogs can clear along the coast due to convection currents formed over coastal slopes. Coastal sailors can frequently foretell imminent sea fog by seeing it forming over coasts before it spreads back out to sea. This fog is not the kind which forms over land during the night and disappears by day. Sea fog can persist for days in some cases.

Element	Trend	Normal change	Normally	Chance of	Possibly
Wind	To come off the sea	Light onshore when morning is sunny	Occurs in the hours before and around lunchtime	Complete calm	Sea fog near fronts, with Force 4–7 winds
Visibility	Fog or mist	50–100 yards over coastal areas, less in banks over sea	Unpredictable, but fog-banks drawn in by sea breeze during the day	10–20 yards	No fog, but generally hazy visibility
Precipitation	Little or none	Drizzle where fog-banks lift over coast and hills	*As for visibility*	Light rain	No precipitation at all
Cloud	Half to full cover	Obscured sky when fog-banks invade	*As for visibility*	Total cover at sea level	No cloud
Temperature	Cool and clammy in fog	From warm and humid to cool and humid	In next few minutes	Cold near the coast all day	Remaining warm
Pressure	Usually no appreciable change				

11 Showers

MAJOR INFERENCE Showers in the next hour or two. They may not be heavy but can be expected to become heavy later. General broken cloud cover of 4–6/8 indicates a sprinkling of shower clouds over level terrain. Showers will grow preferentially over hills and die out in the lee of them. If showers are indicated, but do not develop, then possibly (a) the surface is cooling, (b) air is drying or (c) the upper air is becoming more stable. Look for the cirrus of another depression that can 'kill off' the showers as it streams in.

MAJOR CLUES 1. Big cumulus, ie distance from the base to the tops is greater than the distance from the base to the ground. **2**. Developing solid heads – no spindly chimneys poking upwards. **3**. No cloud layer above to inhibit upward growth. **4**. Cool polar airstream with wind speed typically Force 3–4.

EXPLANATION The classic scenario of a showery airstream is the unstable north-westerly which arrives behind major depressions. Its showers form primarily on windward-facing coasts and the hills inland. The shower activity decreases the further one gets from the windward-facing coasts, but showers frequently sweep right across such comparatively narrow lands as the British Isles. Early growth of ragged cumulus (ie by 0900–1000 GMT) and a cool blustery wind are signs of a showery day to come.

Element	Trend	Normal change	Normally	Risk of	Possibly
Wind	Normally NW or W, marked diurnal variation	Gusty in afternoon, less at night	Diurnally	Force 6–7	Force 2–3 when showers are heavy with thunder
Visibility	Very good	Very good by day, except in showers, bright stars at night	Diurnally	Dawn fog in sheltered industrial areas	Good all night if wind stays up
Precipitation	Rain, snow, occasional hail	Increase with day, die out in the evening	Diurnally	Occasional thunder, especially over hills	Continuous showers over the sea
Cloud	6–7/8 Cb and Cu	No early cloud, maximum shower cloud in middle of day, dying out with evening	Diurnally	Thunderstorms	6–8/8 Sc when air is stabilising
Temperature	Cool	Cold at night, cool during the day	Diurnally	Frost in sheltered spots at night	
Pressure	Steady or rising slowly	High pressure	Over days	Rapid rise and subsequent fall	Slow fall

12 Air mass trough

MAJOR INFERENCE Showers and some more continuous rain, possibly some thunder and gusting winds. Expect the whole thing to be over in an hour or so but do not expect a major change of weather type. Cool showery weather is to be expected after the trough, as it is before it. It is not like a front, which separates different air masses.

MAJOR CLUES **1.** Little cloud ahead of trough in clear polar airstream. **2.** Obvious line of shower and other clouds moving from windward. **3.** Some backing in the wind direction (veering in Southern Hemisphere). **4.** Showers and cloud clear quickly behind the trough, skies clear and winds veer and decrease.

EXPLANATION The cool Polar maritime airstream breeds air mass troughs. Sinking air ahead of (and behind) the trough leads to fewer showers than would be expected in these areas, and may lead to the suspicion that an as yet invisible trough is somewhere upwind. A band of heavy, showery rain passes with the trough and there is a risk of thunderstorms, hail and even waterspouts or tornadoes. Gusty winds of double the mean wind speed occur as the trough passes.

Element	Trend	Normal change	Normally in	Risk of	Possibly
Wind	Force 3–5, westerly	Squally, Force 4–6 W–NW	Half an hour to an hour	Gusts of Force 7 or 8	Veering Force 3–5 NW
Visibility	Very good	1–2 miles in showers	Half an hour to an hour	Less than ½ mile in snow	Very good
Precipitation	Fair or fine	Showery, rain or snow	Half an hour to an hour	Thunder	Fair or fine
Cloud	2–4/8 Cu, 3,000–5,000 ft	7–8/8 Cu, Cb and As. Lowest base 1,000–2,000 ft	Next half hour	Temporarily very low base in snow	2–6/8 Cu or Cb
Temperature	Cool for time of year	Temporarily colder	Next half hour		Cool again
Pressure	Falling slightly	Small fall	Half an hour to an hour	Sharp fall in worst cases	Slow rise

13 Cumulonimbus

MAJOR INFERENCE Showers and/or thunderstorms with heavy rain and perhaps hail. A major storm area possibly lies hidden behind the more obvious clouds.

MAJOR CLUES **1**. Large, solid cloud tops growing upward, but separated (compare 8). **2**. Much surrounding cloud, which is relatively low (compare 12). **3**. Other signs of a polar airstream.

EXPLANATION Individual cumulonimbus clouds may exist over summer cornfields, or over winter snow cover, or wedged in between smaller cumuliform clouds in cool, unstable airstreams at any time of year. They may blow by quickly in breezy airstreams, give a couple of claps of thunder and be gone. In summer the situation depicted may presage the development of a more major storm area, but in this particular case there is little of the attendant dark cloud masses that go with big thunderstorms. The weather type differs from that of 8 by being relatively cool and not sultry. Here the cloud cells are well separated from their neighbours so that showers are also well separated and any thunder that may occur will be relatively insignificant.

Element	Trend	Normal change	Normally over in	Risk of	Possibly
Wind	Light wind possibly toward storm in worst cases	Squally, gusts to 30–40 knots in worst cases	½–2 hours	Tornadoes or waterspouts	Force 2–4 from another direction
Visibility	Moderate	Temporarily poor in precipitation	½–2 hours	Less than ½ mile in snow showers	Moderate to good
Precipitation	Fair or fine	Heavy showers of rain or snow	½–2 hours	Hail and thunder	Fair or fine
Cloud	2–6/8 Ac and As, Cu	6–8/8 Cu and Cb with As and Ci		Funnel clouds	2–6/8 Cu
Temperature	Cool	Cold in showers	½–1 hour		Cool
Pressure	No appreciable change			Moderate fall	

14 Quiet evening

MAJOR INFERENCE A calm night with fog and mist patches, especially in industrial areas and in hollows, river valleys etc. Possibly air and ground frost.

MAJOR CLUES 1. Lack of wind both at the surface and aloft. 2. Strongly stabilising air near the ground causing formation of mist and smoke decks. 3. Little or no low or medium cloud to prevent radiation from the ground.

EXPLANATION The smoke deck shows how rapidly the earth is cooling and so stratifying the air layers over it. The smoke is trapped in an 'inversion' where cool air changes to warmer air above it. This inversion layer will move upward as the night progresses and trap water vapour and smoke near the ground, so leading to mist and fog. If the ground falls below freezing then the fog risk is less as some of the moisture is now held in suspension as solid ice crystals on grass etc. The upper cloud is largely spread-out vapour trails, but they are dense and persistent. There seems, however, to be no organised wind direction at their level and this points to a continuation of the present quiet weather.

Element	Trend	Normal change	Normally over by	Risk of	Possibly
Wind	Calm	Very light offshore land breezes near coasts, especially in the autumn	Midnight	Total calm	Wind picking up before dawn
Visibility	Decreasing	Variable mist and fog	Midnight or early hours	Less than 20 yards	Increasing if wind picks up
Precipitation	No true precipitation	Dew and hoar frost	Early hours	Icy patches on roads	No frost
Cloud	Dispersing	Clear skies	Evening	Increase with the night	8/8 low St, 4–6/8 Sc or increasing Ci
Temperature	Falling	Fall to ground frost and air frost in winter half of year	Dawn or before	Air frost in winter	No frost even in winter if wind and cloud increase
Pressure	Generally steady, possible slight changes, rising or falling			Fall later in night if depression approaching	

Red sky at night

MAJOR INFERENCE The night will be clear and the temperature will drop. The fractostratus clouds below the main cloud base indicate that the air at this level is still wet from the rain falling out of the clouds above, which were associated with a cold front. This wetness left on the ground in the evening and the fall of wind speed with the night may well produce mist and fog patches in areas sheltered from the wind. Frost can also occur in the winter half of the year.

MAJOR CLUES 1. Good expanse of upper cloud on which the sun can project red rays. **2**. Immediate past history of cold front or occlusion (rain, showers, low cloud etc). **3**. Well-broken skies behind the front.

EXPLANATION The low sun of sunset (or sunrise) projects red rays. These do not of themselves presage a fine night. However, a fine night will follow in the example shown in the photograph because the sun can only illuminate the windward clouds if there is no cloud cover over the horizon (ie to windward at sunset). These conditions are fulfilled when a cold front has just passed and Polar air is moving over the observer. It will then be a fine night. Reverse the situation and you have the dawn of a bad day. The sun is now to leeward and shining over a clear horizon onto the clouds of a warm front whose weather and wind has yet to come and is that of which shepherds warn.

Element	Trend	Normal change	Normally over by	Chance of	Possibly
Wind	Decreasing	W to NW, Force 2–3. Calm in sheltered areas	Early hours of morning	Calm by dawn	Increasing again by dawn
Visibility	Decreasing	Mist and fog in sheltered surrounding areas	Early hours of morning	Less than 50 yards in smoke	Clear all night if wind stays up
Precipitation	None, but perhaps ground frost	Hoar frost by dawn in winter half of year	Dawn	Air frost in winter and spring	None if wind stays up
Cloud	Decreasing	Clear skies	Midnight	8/8 low cloud when wind stays up and ground is left moist	Cloudy aloft by dawn if another front on the way
Temperature	Falling sharply	Cool but clear	Dawn	Very low in winter	Little change if wind stays up
Pressure	Rising	Steady rise		Sharp rise and signs of fall by dawn	Little change

Cirrus foretelling improvement

MAJOR INFERENCE The centre of a depression has passed eastwards and so the weather should improve with the wind decreasing, possibly only slowly, while pressure should be rising, possibly rapidly. A risk of showers by day, but there will be clear skies by night over land. Possibly showers day and night over the sea.

MAJOR CLUES Fronts have recently been affecting the area. Now we are watching the rear of a cold front, which we hope is the last of the rain, and will be followed by better weather. However, allow for the possibility that the weather will close in again if there is a second front following this one, which can sometimes (although infrequently) happen.

EXPLANATION In this picture we are standing with the wind blowing from the north-west into our backs. Is this going to be a real improvement? It will be if the high cirrus cloud scudding along the cloud-edge is moving towards the southwest. Now the Crossed Winds Rule for improvement is obeyed and so there should not be any more trouble as the pressure rises. (In other situations, where fronts are appearing to clear, you can in the same way get a better idea of what is happening downwind from the motion of the cirrus compared to the flight of cumulus or other low clouds.)

Element	Trend	Normal change	Normally over in	Risk of	Possibly
Wind	Slow decrease	Force 3–5 by day. Force 2–4 at night	One day	Increase later when pressure rises rapidly	Squally in showers
Visibility	No great change	Obeys diurnal variation	Half a day	Fog and mist by night in sheltered industrial areas	Very good
Precipitation	Showers by day	Clear by night over land. Showers both day and night over the sea		Frost at night in winter half of year	No showers
Cloud	Decreasing	Diurnal variation of Ci or Cb cloud	Half a day	Increase of cirrus later if another front on the way	
Temperature	Cooler	Diurnal variation over land		Freezing	
Pressure	Rising	Rising slowly for real improvement	A day or two	Rapid rise and later rapid fall	Little change if depression weak

17 Will it thunder?

MAJOR INFERENCE Thunderstorms are normally associated with heat and humidity – with a closeness of the atmosphere and a general feeling that storms are not far away. However, there are several different types of storm situation. The one that goes with this sky occurs well above the surface when, as here, clouds of the medium levels grow castellated tops, showing that the air up there is unstable from hot ground and will make the atmosphere prone to producing storms through some depth. Such medium-level storms (when they occur) will often be spectacular with a lot of cloud-to-cloud lightning.

MAJOR CLUES The cloud-type in the foreground is called altocumulus castellanus and it only needs a nudge of heat and humidity to grow into medium-level thunderstorms. However, looking into the distance, we see a more usual form of this cloud. Note the way the clouds form in lines of heap-cloud elements, which is typical. Sight of this form of sky should make you seek a forecast as the storms it foretells may not break out until some hours have passed (if at all).

EXPLANATION Use the sight of this sky with castellanus and floccus (the latter looking like a flock of sheep grazing in a blue sky) to warn of coming thunder – although even the professionals will probably not know exactly when or where it will occur.

Element	Trend	Normal change	Normally over	Risk of	Possibly
Wind	Will remain in same direction, but increase a little	Force 2–4, gusty and perhaps variable	In a few hours	Thunder if surface wind backs	Passing, and later fine
Visibility	No great change	3–6 miles by dawn	During night	1–2 miles in places	No change if wind increases
Precipitation	Little or none	Few thunder spots, if any	During next few hours	Thunderstorms at medium level if wind backs	None at all
Cloud	Not much change	6–7/8 thundery Ac, and As with Cc and dense Ci	In a few hours	8/8 thundery Ac if wind backs	Clearing to 2–4/8 Ac and As
Temperature	Falling	Slight fall			
Pressure	Slight fall	Fall by less than 1 mb in 3 hours	During next few hours	Falling again later, hence deterioration with risk of thunder	Rising, and so major improvement

18 Will it rain?

MAJOR INFERENCE Dark skies with hard-looking bases do not often rain despite their ominous appearance. This is especially so when chinks of sunlight get through the overcast. Another clue is formed by the cloudbase exhibiting downward lumpiness. If the cloudbase loses its hard appearance then expect that rain is falling up there and so allow for it reaching the ground soon.

MAJOR CLUES A large low-cloud area whose base is solid and lumpy will rarely rain. Look for islands of the cloudbase losing their hardness. It is from these islands that rain is beginning to occur. Look for dark bits of cloud forming below the main cloudbase (pannus, 5) that indicate rain beginning to fall at altitude. Look for reduced visibility in any direction, which may indicate that rain is already occurring there.

EXPLANATION On the whole for rain to occur the air must be rising. So sight of a cloud base with downward protuberances is against rain. These protuberances are most obvious when we see mamma. These clouds resemble cow's udders and are at their most pronounced in association with the tornadic storms that occur in the American Midwest. They are not so often seen in Europe and when they are it will be ahead or beyond the cumulonimbus of major thunderstorms. Frontal cloud areas take a long time to disperse (by a process called frontolysis). On the other hand, old fronts may occasionally rejuvenate and rain or showers break out where none were expected.

Element	Trend	Normal change	Normally over	Risk of	Possibly
Wind	To veer and increasing slightly	Veer behind the front; strongly stabilising air (Sc) indicates no great increase in speed	Within next half an hour	A few gusts	In areas prone to them pronounced mamma may indicate tornadoes
Visibility	Increasing	5–10 miles	Next hour or so	Decrease after nightfall	
Precipitation	Little or none	A light shower, possibly just a few spots of rain	Next half an hour	A heavier shower if whole cloud base is not hard	No rain at all, but take note of above remarks concerning tornadoes
Cloud	Decreasing	Fair or fine	An hour or so	4/8 Cu or Cb during afternoon if front clears in forenoon	7/8–8/8 Sc later
Temperature	Little change	Diurnal variation			Cooler
Pressure	Rising	Rising slowly	Next 6 or more hours	Falling later if another depression is on the way	No change

19 Fair weather cumulus

MAJOR INFERENCE Fair weather and light to moderate winds. Seabreezes developing with the day near coasts in spring and summer and, perhaps, penetrating tens of miles inland, as well as the same distances out to sea.

MAJOR CLUES 1. Cumulus clouds that have flat bases and subdued tops. **2**. Distance from base to top less than distance from base to surface. **3**. Ranged in ranks or streets. **4**. Clear area to seaward indicates seabreeze over this area.

EXPLANATION We are inland looking towards the sea, which is about 10 miles away. Looking under the line of cloud in the background we see a clear slot with no clouds. That line is a seabreeze front moving in from the coast – the mechanism of the breeze has led to air sinking over the coast and eroding the clouds there, leaving it sunny. It will soon be completely sunny here as well.

NB On good seabreeze days (typified by the early morning wind being light to moderate, partly unstable airstream with half the sky or less covered in cumulus) the onshore seabreeze cannot be used with the Crossed Winds Rules.

Element	Trend	Normal change	Normally	Chance of	Possibly
Wind	Diurnal variation	Force 2–3 by day. Force 1–2 by night	In a day	Sea breeze	Force 4–5 on the edges of anticyclones
Visibility	Good	Follow diurnal variation, but rarely less than several miles	In a day	Haze inland	Poor locally at night in the winter half of year
Precipitation	None			Showers over hills	
Cloud	Diurnal variation	3–6/8 small Cu by day, little cloud at night	In a day	6/8 Cu along sea breeze fronts	No cloud over coasts
Temperature	Diurnal variation	Maximum by early afternoon. Minimum by dawn	In a day		
Pressure	Steady or rising	Slow rise	In hours or days	Falling when low is encroaching	

20 Cirrus revealing no change

MAJOR INFERENCE The situation will remain largely static, with no marked deterioration or improvement, because the upper wind (revealed by the trailing fallstreaks) and the lower wind (indicated by the way the low clouds lie in lines more or less parallel with the fallstreaks) are shown to be in roughly the same direction. If there is to be a marked change of air mass then the upper and lower winds must be crossing one another at a large angle.

MAJOR CLUES **1.** Cirrus, which might mean the onset of a warm front, but the parallel winds tell of no great change. **2.** No other obvious signs of trouble, such as tumbling barometer.

EXPLANATION A sky with cirrus in it may mean many things. Photographs 1, 2 and 16 show how to sort out some of the messages. There is undoubtedly some wind aloft and that might mean some increase at the surface later. No warm front is indicated downwind so whatever happens it cannot be very bad. Care must be taken to monitor the surface wind direction because on the back of a ridge of high pressure upper and lower winds can be parallel. As the ridge moves over, however, the surface wind backs and so becomes crossed to the upper wind, which probably will not change its direction much. Now a deterioration is on the way!

Element	Trend	Normal change	Normally over	Risk of	Possibly
Wind	Little change	Force 2–4 by day over land	In some hours	Force 4–7 if surface wind backs later	Little change
Visibility	Little change	10 miles or more as wind freshens	In some hours	Deterioration at night	Little change
Precipitation	None				
Cloud	Increasing aloft	3–6/8 Ci and Cs with some Ac and As	In some hours	Total cover of high and medium cloud	No great increase
Temperature	Slight decrease	Cooler due to wind increasing	Soon	Colder in winter	Little change
Pressure	Little change				

21 Stratocumulus

MAJOR INFERENCE No change of weather type yet. Sometimes stratocumulus (Sc) may run ahead of bad weather, but not often. Stratocumulus in the centre of winter anticyclones can accompany the worst of fogs, so in this case it goes hand in hand with a bad weather type. Yet it is a cloud of a largely unchanging situation. Winds are normally light to moderate and shift direction, but not very rapidly.

MAJOR CLUES **1**. Flattened cumuliform elements in large pieces with some lighter chinks between the elements. **2**. Airstream is generally stable, ie no real shower clouds (cumulus or cumulonimbus). **3**. Often accompanies tropical airstreams, which have dried out and the Sc then 'fills in'. **4**. Does not normally attend a bad weather system except on its periphery.

EXPLANATION Looking east over the Cambrian mountains, this stratocumulus formed under high pressure and indicates an airmass is stable.

Sc forms under inversions. It may have been cumulus that has tried to grow through an inversion and has only succeeded in flattening sideways under it. This is the way clear mornings sometimes become totally cloudy. Such inversions are relatively strong, but benign, as depicted here. Sc is a normal accompaniment to a modified Polar airstream that has travelled a long way and in which air from aloft has subsided to produce the inversion. In association with nimbostratus in bad weather Sc may form extensively below the main cloud base so that three cloud decks appear; a low cover of pannus **5** topped by a total cover of Sc above, which hides the really thick rain-bearing Ns clouds.

Element	Trend	Normal change	Normally	Chance of	Possibly
Wind	Little change	Force 2–4 by day. Force 1–3 by night	Diurnally	Calm	Picking up from new direction if a low is encroaching
Visibility	Decreasing	5–8 miles	Diurnally	10 yards in smoke in winter half of year	Smog in industrial areas in winter
Precipitation	None				
Cloud	Variable	6–8/8 Sc sometimes, but may break to 1–3/8 at times	In hours	Total cover in winter with fog	Variable, with clearances and then clouding again
Temperature	Little change	Remaining relatively warm		Cool in fog	Cold in winter
Pressure	Little change	Slow rise or fall	In days	Sharp fall if depression threatens	

Stratus

MAJOR INFERENCE A warm moist tropical maritime air mass. With a relatively strong wind, low stratus is frequently found to the rear of active warm fronts, ie in the warm sectors of young and active depressions. If you see it forming in the evening expect total cover as night begins to fall. Bad for aircraft movements and hill walking.

MAJOR CLUES **1**. Undefined and amorphous base – often covering whole sky. **2**. Airstream moist and muggy. **3**. Accompanied by drizzle when at its wettest, but not normally by rain, except on windward-facing hill slopes.

EXPLANATION A grey and featureless day. Stratus is low and formless – it is fog raised above the earth's surface. It also forms in the easterly winds to the north of depression centres and may obscure the sky on days when thunderstorms are going to erupt later. It must have rain or drizzle falling into it to keep it fuelled and prevent it from breaking up when winds are strong to gale.

Element	Trend	Normal change	Normally in	Risk of	Possibly
Wind	Little change for hours at least	Veer and gust at cold frontal passage	Hours or days	Failing light, when stratus will become fog	Dispersing if wind increases
Visibility	Poor but variable	½–2 miles	Periods of hours or minutes	50 yards if wind lessens	
Precipitation	Drizzle, rain over hills	Unpredictable drizzle patches especially near windward coasts, continuous rain over hills	Tens of minutes to some hours	Rain and showers if near depression centre	No drizzle or rain in less wet airstreams
Cloud	Overcast	8/8 St at 100–300 ft, 8/8 Sc or Ns above	Unpredictable times	Sky obscured and thick fog	2–6/8 Sc or other low cloud if wind increases
Temperature	Muggy	Warm for time of year if cloud breaks	Unpredictable times	Cool or cold under total cover	Hot or warm if cloud breaks
Pressure	Steady or falling	Moderate or slow fall then rising	Hours or days	Falling rapidly if depression centre not yet passed	Rising if centre has passed

23 Altocumulus and cirrocumulus

MAJOR INFERENCE Cirrocumulus (Cc) and altocumulus (Ac) sheets indicate a generally unstable tendency associated with air layers that are being lifted upwards. They often accompany some high-level frontal activity, or they may be due to the general edging up of the high layers when a heated land surface forces the lower layers to expand. 'Mackerel sky, mackerel sky. Not long wet, and not long dry' may accurately sum up these clouds.

MAJOR CLUES **1**. Areas of closely-packed globular elements. **2**. Cirrocumulus has no shadows, altocumulus has light shading. **3**. Often Ac shows coloured patches when illuminated by sun or moon. **4**. Increasing amounts signal a possible deterioration, decreasing amounts indicate a probable improvement.

EXPLANATION Unstable cloud elements at high and medium levels when orientated for deterioration across the surface wind can mean that rain will be locally heavy. In this photograph the Crossed Winds Rules indicate that there is no great change to be expected for some hours at least, because the surface wind is parallel to the major cloud features aloft.

Element	Trend	Normal change	Normally	Risk of	Possibly
Wind	Increase later	Increase somewhat when preceding fronts	In hours	Major increase later	Little change
Visibility	Moderate or good		Diurnal variation		
Precipitation	Intermittent later	Rain, with a thundery tendency later	In hours or may be a day or more	Heavy rain if wind backs	Remaining fair
Cloud	2–6/8 Ac and Cc	3–6/8 Ac and As, with Ci and Cc	In next few hours	8/8 thundery As and Ac later	Cloud decreasing
Temperature	No great change	Diurnal variation	Diurnal variation but cooler if rain comes	Cold in thundery rain	Becoming warm
Pressure	No great change	Fall or rise by small amounts	In hours or days	More rapid fall later if depression approaching	Rising for better weather

24 Coastline clouds

MAJOR INFERENCE Those who live near the coastline know how different the weather and wind over the sea may be to that experienced over the land. Along the coast shown in the photograph we see an example of this often abrupt change. The sea is a great reservoir of heat and so coastal dwellers have much warmer winters than those who live inland. However, early spring is the change-over time as the waxing sun warms the land while the sea becomes close to its lowest temperature. Thus spring is the time of greatest temperature difference and seabreezes can penetrate tens of miles inland and can stem and reverse quite substantial offshore winds (ie blowing from land to sea). The relative warmth of the sea compared to the land in winter can prompt big coastal showers when inland it is quite dry.

MAJOR CLUES 1. Definite and obvious change of cloud conditions near the coastline. **2**. Wind blowing mainly parallel to or off the coast in a showery situation; but blowing onshore without cloud over coast or sea in seabreeze, see 19. **3**. Knowledge of probable sea temperature and air temperature helps to decide likely conditions outside.

EXPLANATION The yachtsman can assess the conditions outside harbour from just inland. Winds increase by 1–2 Beaufort Forces, or more, when they leave the shelter of land. Take maximum gust speed in the harbour to be representative of the mean wind at sea and reef accordingly.

A coastline may form a zone of change as follows: **1**. Unstable air over the sea, but stable over the land (as shown here). **2**. Air stable over sea, but unstable over land. If the wind is parallel to the coast, or blowing offshore, then the reverse can occur; cloud over land but none over sea.

Element	Trend	Normal change is to	Normal times	Risk of	Possibly
Wind	Increasing, gusty at sea	Force 3–4 over the land to 4–5 over the sea	On reaching water with open sea fetch	Force 6, with gusts to 7 or 8	Force 2–3 over land and 3–4 over the sea
Visibility	Poor in showers at sea	6–10 miles out of showers to ½–3 miles in showers	Showers arrive and pass in minutes	Less than ½ mile in snow showers	Over 30 miles
Precipitation	Showers of rain or snow over sea	Infrequent showers inland and frequent showers over sea and immediate coastal strip	On leaving coastal strip for sea	Hail and thunder, but passing	Frequent showers over land and few over sea
Cloud	2–4/8 big Cu and Cb over land, 4–7/8 Cu and Cb at sea	Seaborne cloud over land when wind shifts off sea, land distribution of cloud found off coast when wind shifts off land	Several hours or more, perhaps rapidly if land strongly heated	Funnel clouds, ie waterspouts over sea	
Temperature	Feels cooler over the sea	From normal for time of year on land to cool in showers over sea, despite higher sea temperature	On entering showery area		

Index